D1525996

Four and Twenty
Blackbirds
Soaring

Books By
LOUIS DANIEL BRODSKY

Poetry

Trilogy: A Birth Cycle (1974)
Monday's Child (1975)
The Kingdom of Gewgaw (1976)
Point of Americas II (1976)
Preparing for Incarnations (1976)
La Preciosa (1977)
Stranded in the Land of Transients (1978)
The Uncelebrated Ceremony of Pants Factory Fatso (1978)
Birds in Passage (1980)
Résumé of a Scrapegoat (1980)
Mississippi Vistas (1983)
You Can't Go Back, Exactly (1988)
The Thorough Earth (1989)
Four and Twenty Blackbirds Soaring (1989)

Bibliography (Co-authored with Robert W. Hamblin)

Selections from the William Faulkner Collection of
  Louis Daniel Brodsky: A Descriptive Catalogue (1979)

Faulkner: A Comprehensive Guide to the Brodsky Collection:
    Volume I: The Biobibliography (1982)
    Volume II: The Letters (1984)
    Volume III: The De Gaulle Story (1984)
    Volume IV: Battle Cry (1985)
    Volume V: Manuscripts and Documents (1989)

Country Lawyer and Other Stories for the Screen by
  William Faulkner (1987)

Stallion Road: A Screenplay by William Faulkner (1989)

Biography

William Faulkner: Life Glimpses (1990)

Four and Twenty Blackbirds Soaring

Poems by
Louis Daniel Brodsky

Timeless Press
Saint Louis, Missouri

Timeless Press, Inc.
10411 Clayton Road
Saint Louis, Missouri 63131

Library of Congress Catalog Card Number: 89-50804

ISBN 1-877770-07-8
ISBN 1-877770-08-6 (pbk.)
ISBN 1-877770-09-4 (tape)
ISBN 1-877770-10-8 (tape & pbk. set)

Designed by Ruth A. Dambach
Southeast Missouri State University
Manufactured in the United States of America

First Edition, First Printing (December 1989)

The author would like to express his gratitude to the editors of the following
magazines for permission to reprint poems that first appeared in their pages:
The Southern Review. ''Guilty Until Proven Innocent,'' ''Joseph K,'' ''Between
Connections''
The Cape Rock. ''Word-Seeds,'' ''The Casket Truck,'' ''Redbuds,'' ''The
Flower Store''
Ball State University *Forum.* ''Running in Packs,'' ''Tortoise and Hare,''
''Buffalo''
The Hiram Poetry Review. ''Sitting in Bib Overalls, Workshirt, and Boots on
the Monument to Liberty in the Center of the Square, Jacksonville, Illinois''
The Kansas Quarterly. ''Parachutes,'' ''An Autumnal''
The American Scholar. ''A Sky Filled with Trees''
The Literary Review. ''Jan's Song''
Harper's. ''Rear View Mirror''
Georgia State University Review. ''Smalltown Origins,'' ''The Motion of
Heavenly Bodies''
St. Louis Country Day School Magazine. ''Balloons''

The following poems have been reprinted in annual editions of *Anthology of Magazine Verse and Yearbook of American Poetry*:

1980 Edition. "Buffalo," "My Flying Machine"
1981 Edition. "Ancestry," "Sitting in Bib Overalls, Workshirt, and Boots on the Monument to Liberty in the Center of the Square, Jacksonville, Illinois"
1984 Edition. "Redbuds"
1989 Edition. "Smalltown Origins," "Balloons"

I am very grateful to Alan F. Pater, editor of the *Anthology of Magazine Verse* series, for having chosen to publish a number of my poems in his annual collections.

Some of the poems in this volume have appeared in different versions in the following previously published books by the author:

The Kingdom of Gewgaw (1976). "Helen Among the 12 Disciples"
Point of Americas II (1976). "My Flying Machine," "Ancestry," "Sitting in Bib Overalls, Workshirt, and Boots on the Monument to Liberty in the Center of the Square, Jacksonville, Illinois"
Preparing for Incarnations (1976). "A Sky Filled with Trees," "Tortoise and Hare," "Buffalo"
The Uncelebrated Ceremony of Pants Factory Fatso (1978). "To His Coy Wife," "The Flower Store," "Running in Packs"
Stranded in the Land of Transients (1978). "The Casket Truck," "Joseph K," "Word-Seeds," "Rear View Mirror"
Résumé of a Scrapegoat (1980). "Breaking Through," "Country Cemetery," "Gulliver's Departure," "Redbuds," "The Isle of Lesbos," "Between Connections"
Birds in Passage (1980). "Jan's Song," "A Sky Filled with Trees," "My Flying Machine," "The Casket Truck," "Word-Seeds," "Buffalo," "The Flower Store," "Rear View Mirror," "Running in Packs," "Ancestry"

This book has been measurably enhanced because of Linda Hermelin's excellent editorial suggestions, Jane Goldberg's precise reading of the text for orthographic accuracy, and Pam Wells' organizing and word-processing skills.

Ruth A. Dambach deserves my greatest measure of gratitude; she is responsible for the exacting and beautiful refinements that distinguish this published book.

For my mother and father,
Charlotte and Saul,
on their golden anniversary
4/12/88

Your love for each other
has been the poetry of my growing up
and of my growing older.

Sing a song of sixpence,
　　A pocket full of rye;
Four and twenty blackbirds
　　Baked in a pie.

When the pie was opened,
　　The birds began to sing;
Wasn't that a dainty dish
　　To set before the King?

Anonymous

I know noble accents
And lucid, inescapable rhythms;
But I know, too,
That the blackbird is involved
In what I know.

Wallace Stevens

But the truth, I would like to think, comes out, that when
the reader has read all thirteen different ways of looking
at the blackbird, the reader has his own fourteenth image
of that blackbird which I would like to think is the truth.

William Faulkner

Contents

IMAGINATION
A Sky Filled with Trees   19
My Flying Machine   20
Guilty Until Proven Innocent   21
Parachutes   22
Composing a Garden Book of Verse   23
I Am the Egg Man   24
Crucifishion   25
Balloons   26

ALIENATION
The Casket Truck   29
Gulliver's Departure   30
On the Origin of Mordecai Darwin   32
Between Connections   34
An Autumnal   35
Joseph K   36
Smalltown Origins   37
Rearview Mirror   38

LOVESONGS
Jan's Song   41
To His Coy Wife   42
Total Eclipse of the Vulcan Sun   43
Word-Seeds   44
A Jan-egyric   45
The Physics of Love   46
In Absentia   47
Mystical Union   48

PART II

POET

Author of the Pentateuch 55
Roads Lined With Windtrees 56
The Motion of Heavenly Bodies 58
The Poet Admonishes Himself 59
Conception on the Road 60
Outpatient 61
Birds, Breezes, and Bees 62
Something 63

THE HEARTLAND

Practitioners of the Vernacular 67
Running in Packs 68
Helen Among the 12 Disciples 70
The Auction 72
The Isle of Lesbos 74
Buffalo 76
Tipton's Hidden Treasures 77
Tortoise and Hare 78

TRANSCENDENCE

Ancestry 81
Intimations in Spring 82
In Bib Overalls, Workshirt, and Boots 84
Country Cemetery 86
The Drift of Things 88
Redbuds 89
Breaking Through 90
The Flower Store 91

Imagination

Alienation

Lovesongs

Imagination

A Sky Filled with Trees

For Stuart and Jeffrey Fabe

Even if a hundred bodhi charms,
    Drooping like plump Buddhas
From pear trees planted in the sky,
    Fell from the ivory heavens
And landed in my open eyes
    Like orient moonfruit,

I doubt if I would realize
    They were tokens of fortune
Meant to keep me alive,
    Not as food to be eaten,
Just by being reminders
    That the mind can harvest the sky.

My Flying Machine

Once again I'm integrated with machinery,
Insulated; my nerves are cables
Stretching from pulley to pulley to aileron
And elevator. My mind is a panel
Crowded with instruments and toggle switches,
A cockpit of fidgeting needles and dials.
My tremulous eyes became gyros
Functioning in vacuums like silent worlds
Turning in space; my ears are tuned
To Pitot-static tubes
That check the speed of dreams along this odyssey.

The same flesh that protects my bones
Stretches over wings and fuselage
Fluting through zones of winds aloft.
This unearthly machine burns my blood,
Exhausts unoxygenated thoughts
And exploded harmonies, accelerates rhyme
Toward selected climaxes in time.
Only my voice, of the elements absorbed,
Remains unchanged and controlled by me;
It flies inside the slipstream
Each song I write leaves in its wake.

Guilty Until Proven Innocent

A red-winged blackbird
Lifts precipitously from a soggy field
Contiguous to vision's periphery,
Swoops into view level with my windshield,
Shimmers before being sucked back miraculously
Just as my fleet vehicle slices in two
Its uncompleted flight pattern.

I cringe at this averted collision,
As if witnessing firsthand
The Hindenburg mooring at Hades' cracking stack
Or Titanic slipping into pelagic oblivion,
And remind myself History's sentries
Guard the front and rear portcullises
Of Time's fortress, not its interior.

This near miss persists fifty miles
Down fear's whisperous labyrinth.
That Fate considered implicating me in murder
Places me in the quizzical position
Of having to compose this brief
For my own defense against a felony
I never even remotely intended to commit.

Parachutes

For my sister Babs
on her 35th birthday

Words suspended from silk chutes
Repousséd against the sky's smooth sides
Float slowly into my mind.
One at a time they land,
Each as graceful as a leopard
Leaping a hundred feet to a standing crouch,
Their fragile patterns intact.

From a distant promontory,
Through binoculars, I view them disrobing,
Removing the harnesses of soaring
Until their sleek suits,
Strewn on the ground, and their slender bodies,
Naked to the cursive bone,
Are all that remain of my euphoric brain-shower.

Only then do I descend
To gather their impedimenta
And retrieve them before chill sets in.
Although little is said between us,
I intuit their ecstasy, yet regret
I'm left with only a free-fallen vision
To reconstruct an entire sky.

Composing a Garden Book of Verse

The cosmic Plowman turns earth
His surging brain keeps heated and moist
Just beneath the surface.
His singing fingers
Disperse word-seeds into furrows,
Cortical fissures, like crimson beads
Slipping from a rosary
Unraveling in a golden breeze.
Coursing back and forth
Between sleep and dreaming,
He hoes them over with gentle strokes,

Then relaxes, waits patiently,
Knowing at unpredictable intervals
Tiny shoots will break through
And enter the air haloing the garden
Shimmering with birth.
In such flourishing climes,
Verse-flowers fructify,
And the mind finds nourishment
To sustain its appetite
As, row by row, ears, eyes, and nose
Collaborate in harvesting the soul.

I Am the Egg Man

In this tiny room,
This nest where each egg
Layed out of the fortuitous union
Of imagination and intellect
Comes to rest on paper, I brood,
Solitudinously hatching the future
In which my progeny will pace,
Prance like dancing guinea hens
And peacocks, and strut fuguelike
Through crepuscular études,
Cockadoodledooing poetics to the moon.

Incubating in this tiny room
By the heat of my clicking typewriter,
My pecking fingertips are chicks
Breaking persistently from their shells.
I envision their offspring
Taking wing, soaring above the roost
Where they were first conceived,
Slanting into the wind,
Rising above my restless fancy
Into the thinner air where metaphors,
Like diving falcons, mate beak to beak.

Crucifishion

Despite all the elusive metaphors
For which he'd ever fished in the Great Abyss,
Caught on his brainhook,
Almost brought up to vessel's edge,
Then fortuitously lost
To slippery, jerking fate-quirks,
He'd never really netted a complete Shape,

But rather dragged onto imagination's deck
At the end of his magic pen's gaff
Phosphorescent approximations
Of shimmering, great-flying Leviathan,
Ichthyosaurus, marlin, narwhal
Persisting beyond Vision's misty focus
As finned rainbows twisting in dripping halos.

Today would be different!
The lure, which for three nights straight
He'd stayed awake designing with dreambeads,
Phoenix feathers, poet-hopes,
And hooks contrived of Tyrannosaurus teeth,
Was now ready for baiting: unflinching,
He slashed the barbs through his wrists and cast.

Balloons

The poem I wrote yesterday
      Was a balloon blown up, knotted,
And tied to a convenient pinnacle,
      Then left overnight.

Today, when I returned
      To admire its sensual design,
Passion that had inflated its shape
      Had escaped; it hung limp,

A victim of intrinsic fissures.
      Its translucent skin
Was opaque, inscrutable, uninviting
      To the eyes' smooth fingertips.

When I tried to revise it
      By unknotting and blowing new life
Into its stretched recesses,
      The vessel exploded in my face,

Scattering tattered images and symbols
      For me to gather up and throw away.
O, to release a balloon
      And be inside as it rises from sight!

Alienation

The Casket Truck

For miles I hover above the highway
In the backwash of a vault company's truck,
Staring at two caskets juxtaposed,
One silver, one bronze.
In the morning sun, the ornate skin
That covers these twin containers
Resembles crinkled foil I've often used
To wrap left-over meat and cheese.

Mesmerized by the sight of these sarcophagi,
And frightened by their stark, funereal obtrusiveness
On an otherwise quiet and private drive,
My mind squirms, turns apprehensively
To Yeats' apples and Sir Thomas Browne;
I feel myself being buried alive
In a catacombed potter's field
Of gurgling intestines lined with urns.

For miles I linger behind the speeding coffins
As if connected by an involuntary curiosity
To confirm their destination is different from mine.
Ahead, my turnoff looms;
Nervously, I watch to see which way
The caisson will go, then exit alone
Toward the River, heading west
Into a raw fog stalking me from above.

Gulliver's Departure

It's so quiet here in Redriff
This fine, pink, spring morning
One might think the entire population
Had died of virulent floating spores
Or rats breeding beneath garbage heaps.

Gulliver paces dusty, cobbled streets
Toward the wharf where ship and crew
Wait to transport his flustered imagination
Away from conformities of church and state.
A sullen face belies his inner excitement

On leaving behind wife, childhood,
And Anglican life for the open sea.
As he passes the cast-iron fence
Outlining a tiny, green cemetery
In lacy design, his spaced mind buckles;

Reflections of his mild mother and father,
Held silently in skeletal suspension
In this earth where his birth occurred,
Gurgle to the surface of his brief reverie.
His weeping disturbs the invisible pool

As he recalls their futile attempts
To guard him against straying from reason,
Deviating from traditional regimen
By administering too gentle punishments.
Remorsefully, he kisses their sweet memory;

His heart breaks with hermetic affection.
Yet, knowing, even as in Youth he'd realized,
Salvation lies in setting sail,
He abandons his melancholia and bolts.
Now the vessel fills his entire vision

With a palpable reality beyond dreams.
He throws up his duffel,
Climbs the hemp rung ladder, and boards.
Within hours he'll be out of land's sight,
Past the lighthouse, over the horizon

Without any identity or forwarding address:
And all his credentials will be invalid,
And all his academic scholasticism passé,
And all his expectations for the future useless,
And all his dreams irrelevant, his fears numb.

Toward this day he's gravitated and schemed,
Laid aside and sacrificed a lifetime
To let the moorings come untied.
Soon the sea will set his mind at ease
As he steers for Lilliput, unsuspectingly.

On the Origin of Mordecai Darwin

He awakens with a start,
Involuntarily debates the dialectic
Of breakfast vs. dressing for work,

Ponders the existential notion
Of shaving his face, brushing teeth
And hair, resuming his daily despair

Symbolized by the texturized polyester
Designer Collection suit he wears
To conceal his simian ethics.

Lingering in his womb-warm bathroom,
Gazing at himself in the mirror,
He deliberates on his amazing state of Grace,

Reflects how evolutionary agents
Have flung him from change to change
Up out of rain forest and jungle

Onto the Plains of Civilization
To perpetuate a higher order
Of negative capability and suspended disbelief.

Soon he'll be engaged in the battle
For survival; rush hour
Will take its toll on impatient strains

Whose inexorable gnawing away
At enfeebled psyches will lead inevitably
To extinction of certain species

To which his genus, Homo sapiens,
Is most apocalyptically susceptible.
Now he leaves his house,

Dragging outdoors private doubts
In his trusty attaché case,
Lumbers toward his car,

And pauses beside a low-limbed oak;
Its wandbranches entrance his spirit.
Transfixed, he stoops invisibly,

Almost bending at the center of his being,
Then begins to locomote on all fours,
Tottering, gaining equilibrium,

Going sideways, beating his chest,
Climbing, brachiating
With vestigial thumbs, prehensile tail.

Suddenly, beneath morning's sun,
He discovers the euphoria of arboreal soaring,
Intuiting in a flash

He'll never again brush his teeth, shave,
Crave meat, pare his toenails,
Or consult the Douay or King James Creation.

Between Connections

The foggy countryside is dotted with waifs
Occasionally penetrating its glued layers
To make connections, locate junctions,
Navigate cloverleafs,
And reach destinations
Somewhere beyond the pervasive gray
That permeates day's escape routes.

These metaphors racing through hollows
Past hedgerows out of sight
Might be rabbits, vehicles conveying people,
Or vessels fleeting through my eyes
Containing placid, passive meanings
Imagination assigns to uprootedness
And evokes in defining dead time.

Regardless, as I wait by the roadside,
My mind refuses to differentiate
One kind of transience from another
Between symbols stopping briefly
Like trains at stations along the brain
To take on and discharge passengers.
Every fragment of the incomplete vision

Has potential to become the one link
That could connect all images
With what I think about my own location;
But none relinquishes its secret
As I stand in plain sight of everyone
In the middle of an inconvenienced identity
Trying to thumb a ride home.

An Autumnal

For Hayden Carruth

Like the edges of bird feathers,
This Septembering air
Is tinged with a definite hint of change
And rich mysteriousness.

I sniff its crisp morning chill;
Wisconsin fills my nostrils.
My eyes become chipmunks
Foraging for memories of summer's events
To hoard against imminent winter,

While the autumnal equinox,
Like a star-crazed tatterdemalion
Hitchhiking into Oblivion,
Evanesces in gentle, sugary opaques.

Even my opalescent children
Have exceeded too quickly
The velocity of vision and insight,
As though the days passed
Were compressed in a necromancer's wand

Waved over their growth
To show them the passage back to God.
I turn toward the mirror of my thoughts
For a reflection, an echo, and balk:

The visage in the glass is a harpy
On a fence, stiff and stark black
Except for the edges of its feathers
Which are tinged with the ochreous scent
Of someone nearby waiting to die.

Joseph K

From dawn through day's inexorable yawning
Into restless nightmare again,
His existence is a prism filled with stills
Attached to an invisibly spinning axle
Fixed in the aimless void of illusion.

Before, he advanced from court to court
Crowded with bemused empty faces.
Obliviously they listened to his piteous appeals
And not-unreasoned pleas of innocence
For ostensible crimes against the psyche.

Yet, his conviction was predetermined;
He never even had a beggar's chance
To free himself from the stigma of martyrdom
With which his habitual and abstemious lifestyle
Had branded his soul in the eyes of his jurors.

Now, constraints levied on his brain
By the unrelenting Draconian executioner
Of his mind's easily-swayed Sanhedrin
Have left him raving in a padded cell,
Beseeching commutation from his life sentence.

Occasionally he steps out of his solitude
For a smoke or scribbles his name in chalk
On the granite walls to reassure himself
He's still there; even as they lead him
Down the dark hall to the stale room,

He repeats his profound litany of innocence.
They strap his legs and white wrists
To the chair; the lights dim into quietude;
His vertebrae fuse, nerves snap.
Returning from his amnesiac journey

To the edge of the sea where sleep flows,
He sits up in bed on numb elbows,
Dumbfounded by the degree of his self-deceit,
Troubled only by not knowing
In which room of the dream he's awakened.

Smalltown Origins

Childhood is the same small town
From which all of us came
Before seeking more sophisticated surroundings
To domesticate our displaced spirits.

It's that vague place in a mid-summer's gaze
We wistfully allude to in dazed years
As the whistle stop named Freedom
Youth's sleek express flew through

Forging toward Wisdom's conventional City
To repeat Sister Carrie's disillusionment,
Or way station at Taylor, Mississippi,
Where Temple Drake prematurely detrained

To rendezvous with her future's undoing.
Childhood is our heart's darling,
Fancy's collective silhouette
Shimmering against senility's dim scrim.

No matter how far we stray
Off the trod path of common circumstances,
We converge on a shared heritage,
Become heirs to, beneficaries of, regret;

We overweigh daydreams
Plotting escapes from bland fantasies,
Conceiving ways of recreating tree houses,
Cowboys, dolls, hide-and-seek epiphanies.

Even as Death designs personalized shrouds
To throw over our drowsy, opaque eyes,
We stroke blankets, suck thumbs,
And nestle Fate's numb, shrunken breast.

Rearview Mirror

When I stare in the mirror too long,
The jagged edges of my reflected identity
Scratch my eyes, make them bleed;
Their lids yellow like wilting orchids.

The strange face pasted to flat glass
Is a gross facsimile of a classroom doll
Cut from rough, colored stock,
A Halloween mask, a shadow puppet,

A fractured Picasso with both eyes
On one side of the nose, and the mustache
Of a Guernica bull rising up
To puncture the skin containing its own image.

Although the portrait has neither signature
Nor date to show its provenance
And destination, I recognize it anyway
By the way it speaks in pantomime

The vocabulary of crow's-feet, double chin,
Ingrown stubble; the phonetics of old age,
Projecting my face on a silvery screen
The size of my confined lifetime,

Recite a dialogue between my eyes
And insight the future casts from backlight
Dripping off the dying afternoon
As the past absorbs me in its lunatic gaze.

Lovesongs

Jan's Song

A loquacious breeze caresses our insides
As twilight scribbles the ears
With spacious elegies.
Ivory sea gulls,
Describing spiral metaphors against the sky,
Collide with our eyes
Swooping aloft from this primal grot.

Last night we inlaid Love's nave
With glowing, gold mosaics,
Sprinkled Coconut Grove with odes.
Today we take up the search for words
To church our dreams
And rhyme us into shimmering wind chimes
Hung from the sun.

To His Coy Wife

I count the cost of being apart,
Even one minute,
In eons of eternity squandered.
Our impermanence is so spendthrift,
Yet calculably precious,
The slightest separation seems exorbitant
When measured against the inexorable Forever.

We can't afford the increased interest
Accruing on interest forfeited
When we withdraw from each other
In vain argument,
Then reborrow love at a higher rate.
Such fluctuations
Debase the pure ingot.

I beg you, Lady, don't remain aloof!
Indebtedness can't bankrupt us.
Invest in me your gentleness,
And I'll remunerate you
From the corpus of my soul's estate.
Just remember, trust earned
Is the currency that will buy us Paradise.

Total Eclipse of the Vulcan Sun

For Janny,
my Diana

Through steamy July's midnight leaves,
You, in blue negligee,
And I, completely nude, stand on the patio
Holding hands,
Observing the full moon succumb by degrees
To the earth's umbra.
Even the naked eye can see it
Slowly metamorphosing from yellow-gold to black
And back like a swarm of grasshoppers
Passing across a wheat field
Three hours wide.

Slugs coursing like ocean going boats
Over concrete moats
Separating our castle from West Columbia
And the rest of the universe
Distract our focus; then, bleary-eyed,
We gaze skyward again
To remind ourselves
Time is one continuous motion, not sequential,
Effacement a temporary phase
In the overall design:
We proclaim our momentariness eternal.

Word-Seeds

For my flower child, Jan

I planted word-seeds
With delicate articulation
Between furrows of teeth and tongue,
Covered them over with subtle persuasion
To keep them deeply penetrated,
Away from scavenging beaks
And sniffing, rodent noses
That might nip meaning in the bud.

Then I waited for their first shoots,
Rooted where the original seeds
Exploded into gentle tendrils,
To pierce my garden's weeded surface
That her eyes might scan
My perfectly slender verses
Rising in bouquets of "I-Love-Yous"
For her ears to arrange in their clear vases.

A Jan-egyric

This glorious morning
Is perfect for exploring euphoria,
Investigating prescience,
Planing the psyche's warped doors
And opening them to fresh insights,
Praising painted turtles
Sunning in prismatic bowls,
Hailing schism, dogma, YHWH,
Metaphors soaring above rhetoric,
And, most importantly, You,
Celebrating You, my blessed Lady.

Without your fidelity
To my oblique ways of reciprocating love,
Changing gold into pyrite,
Letting sweet Chablis vinegar my tongue,
And lacking your compassion
To forgive promises made
In the heat of poetic creation
And disavowed when the spell dissolves,
I would celebrate life
As one continuous exhalation,
An uninspired exercise in dying.

The Physics of Love

For Jan, at 39

The whole notion of epiphany, apotheosis
Is rolled up in a Marvell-ball
Called Love
Screaming toward us, seizing our eyes,
Gathering up our lives in its forward motion.

We neither demur nor encourage
The blessed volitionlessness of our magnetics,
But blindly worship vital dynamics
That shape from space poetic tropes
In which we clothe our naked hopes and dreams.

Curiosity, delight, sensual wonderment
Are placebos low-flying deities prescribe
To placate our primal needs
While treating us with paradisiacal elixirs
To free our earthly senses.

As one sum, we two have become indivisible
By all attractive numbers.
Uniquely we've discovered *the* formula:
Tenderness^2 multiplied by Trust
Equals Time to its highest power, Eternity.

In Absentia

Although our separations
Grow consistently more attenuated
And increasingly frequent,
We need not be concerned;

They strengthen our resolution
To cherish interludes,
Share their heritage of moments and glances
That entrance the spirit,

Regardless how evanescent
And frangible. No amount of hours
Or years spent in cloisters
Of mere familiarity,

Or in the convent's silent cubicles
As conjugal bed partners
Indentured to a matrimony
Consisting of lip-service rituals,

Can approximate the intensity
Generated by a solitary kiss
We give each other
When returning from our worlds apart.

Indeed, blessed mistress and wife,
By these extended interruptions,
You and I may be making
Sage preparations

For best enduring and outlasting
Death's berefting of our physical selves.
Eternity might require of us
Loving that leaps eons and galaxies.

Mystical Union

For loving Jan
on the 11th evolution
of our wedding

Eleven years ago this moment,
Ocean and Land joined hands;
The Sky held its breath
While you and I, Jan,
Celebrated our own fusion of souls and bones
In San Francisco's misty Sutro Park.

That cornflower morning,
You, draped in antique crocheted lace —
A nymph borne of that glorious day —
And I, in workshirt, jeans, and boots,
Swigged Chianti,
Pinched hunks of raisin bread

From a freshly baked loaf,
Exchanged "forever afters" with our eyes
And nervous laughter; we tasted grace!
O, that irretrievable "just yesterday"
Seems so terribly recent,
Yet so impalpably far, far away

From where we sit this distant noon,
Sipping Chablis at a patio café
In midtown St. Louis,
Reminiscing in gentle, dizzy whispers
About our marriage ceremony
And its sacred, pagan rites.

The hiatus between now and then
Seems an endless instant
When remembered from paintings and poems
Created in our home on West Columbia
We'd blended with the innocence of children
And adult accomplishments

Meant not to indenture, but free us
From conventions that enslave head and heart.
With brief grief rising to exultation,
We toast *that* mystical moment and *this*,
Knowing Sky, Land, and Ocean
Still worship our Sutro elopement.

PART II

Poet

The Heartland

Transcendence

Poet

Author of the Pentateuch

Alone, as always,
I heed my solitudinous calling
By reaching for pen and ledger book
In which to record the momentary stirrings
My words create
Giving birth, nursing,
Weaning their progeny, Poetry.

No matter where I sojourn,
Forebears and scions
Find me resigned to timeless contemplation,
Recognize in me their Songmaker
Composing sky and trees into rhapsodies,
Exploding odes from lullabies:
Mystical whispers of kissing gods.

Whether patriarch, baby, middle-aged,
Father or Son (simultaneously One),
I sign my name in lamb's blood
And rediscover daily
My reason for reigning over,
While remaining subservient to, the senses:
I am the tribal scribe

Whose earthly curse —
Transubstantiating into verse
Expiations my unholy soul rehearses —
Also is the purpose of my paltry life,
The hallmark that distinguishes dying.
Why else would I worship writing
With such unmerciful determination?

Roads Lined With Windtrees

For Jan, Trilogy, and Troika,
my blessed Trinity

Vague strains sing me awake,
Redeem silence from brooding and fatigue
This interminable drive south.
My heart, miming the melody,
Creates an unsuspected convergence,
Stirs the blood of otherworldly stimuli.

Edging ever farther from home,
I close the distance separating loneliness
From those who've saved me
Suffering cosmic desolation
By listening to and memorizing the breeze
Streaming past my speeding contours.

Suddenly, I see my boy Troika and Miss Trilogy
Behind voices inside the wind;
Their breathless, measured cadences
Inspire me to such sweet forgetfulness
Dislocation ceases seizing me,
Disturbing equilibrium. I surface

As if from a deep, Dead Sea sleep,
Myself, my spirit, a vibrating diapason
Spiraling along a double-helix highway,
Traversing an endless clef
Back and forth, gaining momentum,
Replicating myself through recreation

Every mile I've strayed since leaving home
To seek the source of Metaphor.
Now I realize the force behind my quest
Has been you, blessed family,
My mission to bring you time-rhymes
From my reclusive soul,

Musical souvenirs — fugues, études,
And scherzos — from my heart's Wailing Wall
Beyond ancient sands Moses roamed.
Only for you, Jan, and for our children
Do I pluck poems from golden windtrees
Growing beside roads only I compose.

The Motion of Heavenly Bodies

Poetic rotation
Is the only motion his psyche knows
Whose twin, spinning dynamos,
Powering hemispherical gyros,
Go from stasis to full speed,
Sleeping to complete dream
Without shifting gears, without moving,

Simply by focusing on the road
That transports his soul from home, Home,
Along free-verse lanes
His abstract passage concretely casts:
Energies orbiting Energy's core
In endlessly bending song.

The Poet Admonishes Himself

After humid June, dry July,
And September's first, thirsting half,
The cruel, fetid days
Begin cooling to soothing hues;
Relief reawakens the battered spirit,
Renews the subdued soul
To primal delight in elemental essences:
Trees, streams, houses being painted,
People taking evening walks,
Children rushing to and from school
Igniting the creative spark
By striking curiosity, intellect, and memory
Against the base flint, ignorance.

With such immediate jubilation,
Who has even a moment to heed omens
Dropped from gnawing squirrels,
Twisting from limbs into brittleness,
Or fluttering earthward
From wing tips bound south out of time?
And who was meant to sequester himself
Brooding over such autumnalities
When Fall's Indian summer
Makes itself so accessible to us all
Just by our calling out its myriad names?
Even the most devoted poet
Should be ashamed to squander energy indoors
Seducing a too accommodating Muse.

"Fool!" I admonish myself.
"Forget despondency!
Exchange your grievances and lethargy
For a swim in the quick-running arteries!"
Ah, what a rush to be floated alive
Toward the core
From whose auricled promontory
Those who crave that free-falling feeling
Of leaving the head through the heart
Leap and soar!

Conception on the Road

The road over which I float
Is a Fallopian tube
Coercing me, coaxing,
Guiding my intellect inexorably higher
Into its sinuous conduit.
I'm a motile sperm
Traveling miles to reach my destination
Somewhere up ahead.

The fluid moving my senses
Is lubricious music
Undulating in rhythmic sympathy
This concupiscent morning.
Whether metaphor awaiting fertilization
Or enigmatic symbol
Quivering with euphoric anticipation
Of being penetrated,

The ovum toward whose shore I soar
With furious determination
Is a uterine core
Capable of procreation.
Suddenly, in one climactic orgasm,
I drive into the sun,
Arrive home with my newborne:
I, a man-child, begetter of poems!

Outpatient

On this warm, autumnal, Farmington morning,
He malingers in the Capitol Café,
Prosaically disentangling
September-ending's suspended metaphors
And dangling participial malaises;
A hobo-poet stowed away in his own rolled bag
Tied to a divining rod
Slung over his bony shoulder,
Still trying to cross the Heartland's Sinai
Without realizing his caravansary
Mired here years ago in living quicksand.

Not like the lunatic Roman moved by sheer beauty
To kiss smooth the rim of his vase,
Nor out of dissolute solitude
Does he bite his coffee cup's rough lip,
Talk to its steaming draught
Lifting above memory's hemispherical peripheries,
But as falconer stroking falcons,
Poised to set free blindered thoughts
Caught in tautologies,
Let them circle on verse-thermals
Soaring toward the eye of the sky's volcano.

Suddenly distracted from implacable distraction,
He gazes up; sane focus
Identifies those loitering in adjacent booths,
Rocking on wobbly stools,
Shoeing time to inaudible music,
Spewing sibilant philippics and jeremiads,
As kindred inmates without cells:
The Capitol Café's regular, paying clientele
On leave to spend or suspend each day
In patient tranquility,
And nothing, nothing but freedom on their hands.

Birds, Breezes, and Bees

How soft and sweet and sleepy the breezes are
This August afternoon
When bees seem to float in endless hovering,
And birds etch the empty air
With operatic posturing; their pastoral songs
Belong to a long-ago effluvium
Suffused with broadcloth pioneers, hearty souls
Willing to partake of Creation's slow unfolding,
If for no other reason
Than that their heritage resembled parched earth,
Not concrete apartments, tarred streets.

I listen too intently; that's my basest fault.
There's no room in my conception of the universe
For mistaken hopes or misleading dreams.
Today's notions of heroics are grossly limited,
Not even whimpers, but knowing silences
Splayed like dim shadows
Across Biafran faces, unspoken grotesqueries
Imagined by the boxcar people huddled in the dark stench
Of their attenuated captivity by the Aryan Pharaoh.
Realizing this, the least imaginative birdcall,
Alliterative breeze, and bee-fluttering

Excites me to life's gentle schizophrenias,
Paroles my sensibilities from fetid incarceration
In musty penitentiaries below the soul.
Today, for some unexplained reason,
I revel in just being here,
An evanescent trespasser, Bedouin pitching tent
On desolate sands my existence describes
In its lunatic pacing. Writing verse
Sustains my pledge to remain faithful
And alert to the birds, breezes, and bees;
They inspire me to exercise my freedom to fly!

Something

For Bob Hamblin,
another way of saying
No! to Death

Something there is
Preternaturally compelling
In the essential genes controlling my mind
That provokes its cortical Sanhedrin
To mandate my hand take up pen
And write; something inscrutable
That resists description, refuses to explain
Why my insatiable psyche
Never seems satisfied just being prolific
Or considers its signature,
Affixed in rhythmic mellifluousness,
Sufficient proof of its sole authorship;

Something mystical, magical,
That would have me rhyme the universe
Into a divine pattern
Indivisible by mere human comprehension
Which, like sheet lightning,
Might play out the entire range of sky
Before discovering its own design;
Something informing my verse chronicle
With my tiny spirit's grandeur;
Something approximating godliness
That reminds me my dying
Shall not be squandered on cosmic silence.

The Heartland

Practitioners of the Vernacular

Anyone, who with a straight face can say,
"I ain't got but one,"
And not suffer the slightest trace of anguish
Or guilt for perpetrating on the language
Heinous effrontery,
Should be struck dumb
By some higher denomination of angels,

Or at least publicly stoned
For condoning metaphorical rape, plunder,
And Visigothic molestation,
Instead of being revered mimetically
By all who would emulate this very pattern
In daily speech, legal disputation,
And pulpit harangue: "Now, ain't that so?"

Running in Packs

I race from a frigid outdoors this morning
Into the spastic blast of a space heater
And take a seat out of its path
As though it might be a laser
About to cut in half my uncaffeinated brain.

The radio is a coop of roosting hens;
A Seeburg Discotheque and cigarette dispenser
Are swayback horses asleep on their feet;
Empty chairs, four to a table,
Are piglets stuck to stolid sows' teats.

Like a child hiding from the universe
Behind hands cupped over his eyes,
I squeeze my lids to pain,
But no transformations transport me:
The Here and Now refuses to dematerialize.

Through jalousies I see splintered dawn
Being steadily carpentered, the sky nailed
Piece by tongue-and-groove piece
Into a partition dividing darkness from light.
Soon the spacious edifice will be built,

Ready for occupancy by waking souls.
But the sharp-edged bark of a dog
Scratching at the café door shatters my image.
I detect eight senators, in bib-togas,
Feed hats, and boots, jeering salaciously,

Their bellies rippling like waves
From a stone thrown into a stagnant pool
By a fool trying to imitate Creation.
At first I lose the implied connection
Between mutt and waitress, who confesses

The stray belongs to her; they discern
Deeper meaning, taller humor in her futility
Shooing it from the entrance, sending it home.
Sodomy polka-dots their obscene grins
And eyes with prurient visions of her nude body

Strenuously mounted by the scraggly cur, her lover.
As she slinks in and out of the kitchen,
They mix whispers with snickers and guffaws,
Sing praises of leading a dog's life,
Testify to letting a sleeping dog "lay,"

Keeping a pet of questionable reputation
Fenced in its cage or tied to its owner's bedpost.
On leaving, I survey the senators and see, instead,
Eight canines, paws on table, tails awag,
Barking insanely at the waning moon.

Helen Among the 12 Disciples

For Margaret and Dick Haxel

Chair legs claw the terrazzo floor
With raw, bawdy screeches
As the men in feed hats take their seats
This autumn-cool, June day.
The blond, rouge-cheeked waitress
With blue mascara eyelids
Wearing too tight jeans
And gauzy blouse over taut breasts
Arouses their sleepy minds,
Brings blood rushing into fat, flat veins.

Like hands groping in the dark,
A babel of undramatic voices
Reaches to touch her white arms.
Dressed, she stands naked before them
In the middle of the cold floor,
Unabashed. They order eggs,
Gravy biscuits, a pot of coffee,
Three fresh plates of gossip,
Then turn momentarily stony
As her bouncing body floats away.

She awakens before five each dawn
To be violated by viperine tongues
And bovine eyes used to guiding sows to troughs.
But their bib-overalled protocol
Has failed to reduce her silky silence
To snide rejoinders and caustic asides.
Just now, she returns with their food,
Flies in and out like a bee
Pollinating their base desires with a smile.
A heifer in heat, she crazies them

Breathing urgent fertility down their spines.
Her few words render each subservient,
As if she were Queen of the Nile
Newly arrived among Bedouins
Thirsting in a wet desert.
With prurient intent all succumb to her beauty.
They would worship her pagan form
Were she not Reverend Brown's eldest daughter,
Helen, the town's notorious whore,
A harlot among disciples of the Lord.

The Auction

Tipton's tight-fisted Wizards of Wall Street
Confer early this Sunday morning
At the Crystal Café
To interpret implications of yesterday's auction
Of Widow Scott's estate.
The Chrysler-Plymouth dealer
Leads the heated debate
Over devaluation of the dollar
And conspicuous consumption characterizing the sale.
He remarks, "You shoulda seed the prices
That damn junk pile of rugs brought,
Even if they was from Persia and Brussels,
17th and 18th centuries."

Another intones, "I bid a hundred-forty
On a parlor stove; it sold for thirty less.
Later, they claimed me owner of a broke TV,
And I hadn't even bid."
A third exclaims, "I saw sets of dishes
Bring six hundred each,
Just because they had gold rims,
Bavaria and Prussia printed on their backs."
"People'r sick," pontificates a farmer.
"An inlaid dining room 'suit,'
Though 'beautyful' equipment,
Went to some young kid I ain't never seed
For thirty-and-a-half hundred beans."

"I'll tell you one thing," adds the pharmacist,
"We need to revise our expectations!
When people can clip food coupons,
Draw stay-home pay through the week,
Then show up Sabbath day and drop a wad
On shit they wouldn't buy at the dime store,
Somethin's wrong. What's the difference
If it says Spoede or Sèvres

*   *   *

Instead of Nippon, Korpa, or Hong Prong?
It's all made by foreign sons-of-bitches anyway!''
"All the power to them what's got it,"
Says the cop. "If I was black and sixty-five,
I'd have it made, too — in the shade!''

"Boys, I've gotta get to church; it's late!''
Collective voices rise like woodsmoke,
Gather in common exhortation:
"Pray for us, Diamond Jim!''
The Chrysler-Plymouth dealer gazes sidelong,
His raised eyebrows shifty as snakes
Slithering away from danger.
He sneers, "Pray for yourselfs, boys.
It's gonna take all I got
Just to persuade God
To renew the loan He made yesterday
So's I could buy one of those ratty rugs
Eunice just *had* to have for our rathskeller.''

The Isle of Lesbos

Air inside the Crystal Café
Is rife with hog-trough badinage.
Just now, debates progress
On the life expectancy of private enterprise
In light of higher taxes,
Probabilities of drought repeating
Last year's debacle, livestock inoculations,

And the inscrutable circumstances
Surrounding Red Brewster's recent suicide.
Speculation runs high
In favor of his wife's estrangement,
Her abrupt separation
To take up residence in Vegas
With a flashy man of vague credentials.

Some say pressure from meeting payments
On term notes for machinery purchased
To make 1,000 acres produce
May have caused the tragedy; others scoff
At the basically weak son-of-a-bitch
They always assumed Red to be
Beneath layers of his humble dignity.

Soon the eulogy for Brewster concludes,
But every head, instead of bowing,
Raises in restless attentiveness
To assay two tourists
Presumably on their way to the Lake.
All eyes are slot machine reels
Lining up on bell-fruits

As one, then the next, recognizes the lady
In scanty pants, dyed-blond hair,
As ill-fated Red Brewster's widow.
Although unable to place her companion,
They observe with growing outrage
Both nonchalantly holding hands,
Brazenly absorbed in their own bold gazes.

And in a moment of utter shock,
Each self-elected arbiter
Of Tiptonian mores, each vigilante
Empowered to safeguard his community
With decency and impunity, awakens
To something never discussed collectively,
The stuff of medieval plagues:

Witch-hunts, inquisitions, autos-da-fé,
Demons invading neighbors' houses,
Poltergeists, succubi
Disrupting the peaceful relationship
Between man and wife in lush Arcady.
Slowly, their hushed tongues
Flicker into laughterless persiflage.

By squeamish degrees the men leave.
But, as if forced to pay homage,
Each must pass the table
Where both ladies
Perpetuate their intimacies unabashedly,
Whispering Lesbian obscenities,
Desecrations the men will decry for weeks.

Buffalo

Its flat, insect-blackened radiator grill
Is a buffalo's nose; twin stacks
Become the rugged creature's glistening horns;
Eighteen spinning wheels are four hoofs
Churning cement plains;
Its screaming, forty-foot trailer
Takes the shape of a humpbacked spine,
Writhing belly, and shaggy hindquarters
Fleshed with iron and corrugated steel.

Whoever said History slaughtered wholesale
All those sons-of-bitches
Had his ear glued to the wrong rail.
Once again, America's prairies are overrun
With hordes snorting diesel exhaust.
A second, greed-inspired massacre
Might indeed be an ecological blessing
Protecting us from being trampled to death
By desperately stampeding bison.

Tipton's Hidden Treasures

The Midwest through which I drive
This too cool June dusk,
Pressing toward Columbia before sunset,
Is at rest; wet fescue
Laced with goldenrod, strafed on jagged wing
By barn swallows collecting insects,
Sets my olfactories on edge:
Its rank, sweet seething is dream-semen
Fertilizing my paradisal eyes with memories.

Rabbits emerging from thick grass
At road's shoulder, red-winged blackbirds
Perched atop its drooping tassels,
"Mushrats" and possums
Occasionally splayed along the winding macadam,
Faint traces of skunk
Staining the fecund air, and grazing cows,
Myriad and stolid, remember my passing face
From summers, decades, generations ago.

I, too, this peaceful evening
Vaguely recall being through here before
On other journeys from waking
Toward sleep, traversing this desolate road
One strut, strophe, foot at a time
On my way from poem, home,
To poem again along the circumference
Of the dome my geodesic imagination measures
That shelters me from Hellstones.

As God's paltry emissary in this gentle emptiness,
I record existing conditions,
Verify His work remains untrammeled
By civilized usurpations.
Satisfied, I write my final line,
Then freeze: off to my right,
Behind cyclone-fenced farmland,
Three white Titans cleaving to slanted gantries
Hold the entire horizon at bay.

Tortoise and Hare

The creaking, two-seat, wood-spoked buggy
From Fortuna, parked on the tarred lot
Of Gerbes Grocery Store, is no metaphor
Or premeditated distortion of minds
Discontented with conventional travel and time,

But rather a ragged pair of nags,
Patient, despite the heat, tails busy with flies,
Letting drop caked manure on the pavement.
They belong to a convent-cloth couple
Who've come twelve miles out of need

From the private, tightly-knit community
Where generations of relatives have settled
In precise continuity with their forebears.
Twice weekly, one family is chosen
To buy foodstuffs for the rest,

Jettison quietude they've maintained outside society
That relies on heavy-duty shock absorbers,
Power steering and brakes, radial tires,
Automatic transmissions, and air-conditioning
To persuade people they're making progress

Escaping sweaty bondage to the past.
Meanwhile, these Amish have made the decades
Slaves to *their* exigencies, teaching trades
To cooper, wheelwright, blacksmith, and farmer,
Refusing to believe every gewgawed thing

Related to change is really worth pursuing,
Or that each newly-contrived, mechanical intrusion
And scientific breakthrough simplifies life.
Creaking, wood-spoked wheels take to the road
Unnoticed, the buggy a chariot flying to God.

Transcendence

Ancestry

I stand knee-deep in the ocean
Examining the tepid, eddying sand
Collecting about my feet like hungry minnows.
These particles are the oldest
That still exist, older than Moses,
Younger only than the planet itself.

My own bones are composed of granules
That once came awash on desert shores.
Is it possible I recognize my ancestry
Beneath these sunny shallows,
Associate refracting shadows with families
Buried a thousand generations ago?

I stoop to pick up a fluted rock
Alive with fossils. I can almost feel worms
Wriggling in my wet palm,
Almost hear its captured voices
Calling me back to the Deep,
Asking me for my body to inhabit again.

Intimations in Spring

I yawn; my spirit stretches
Beneath its taut flesh
As if in the inchoate throes of molting.

Indeed, on this warm morning,
Lush and fecund as teenage girls
Flaunting buxom breasts,

I realize how precious, yet precarious,
My connection is to the quick
And to souls no longer existent.

It must have something to do
With the birds' rhythmic stichometry
Amidst thick twigs;

Something about wet grass
That outglistens cut-glass vases
And multifaceted diamonds;

Something in the ecstasy
My young daughter, Trilogy, exudes
Arcing recklessly in her swing

Through the too humid April air
Before we leave for school
(O, her blessed innocence of finalities,

Who asks me why the trees
Aren't loading up
With any colors "besept" green

As in autumn they do, falling)
That brings me so early
To the brink of thinking's magical pool

To drink in its mystical truth
And get drugged...and get crazy
On the pure, pristine perfection of Beauty

That has nothing to do
With human formulation, but rather waits
To be seen, to be heard, to be entered

By the most brainless creatures,
As well as lowliest poet,
In order to complete its own metamorphosis

And be possessed by those few
Who would get close enough to its core
To see God watching them.

Something this morning convinces me
My spirit has already outgrown its mortality
And is about to soar.

In Bib Overalls, Workshirt, and Boots

*Sitting on the monument to Liberty in the
center of the Square, Jacksonville, Illinois*

"The mystic chords of memory, stretching from
every battlefield to every patriot heart and hearth-
stone over all this broad land, will yet swell the
chorus of the Union when touched as they surely
will be by the better angels of our Nature."

Abraham Lincoln

The names of those who fought
And died in civil strife
Are inscribed around the pedestal
Atop which I slouch
Watching anonymous townsfolk on foot,
In vehicles entering the Square,
Hurriedly circling, leaving, returning,
Retreating like blood coursing toward death.

I imagine them in blue uniforms,
Cap, scabbard, and bayonet,
Marching for a common cause to uncommon tunes.
But the vision shatters into pieces:
Ordinary citizens
Pursuing personal liberties, individual freedoms,

While the disembodied names
Raised slightly on bronze plaques
Turn black-green, crack, snap
From municipal neglect and weathering.
Vigorously, as Aladdin,
I rub my shirttail across the lackluster letters;
A kind of static magic
Brings images back from shadow.

No longer doomed to outlast in exile
The memory of their deeds,
Voices beneath the granite base
Come unentombed from ageless incarceration:
They form a chorus only I can hear this Easter,
Resurrection, of a sort, for a non-believer!

Country Cemetery

Just off Highway 50,
Two miles east of Tipton
Down a gravelly road dividing cows
From wheat, corn from more corn,
The Midwest lies at rest.

Tin windmills,
Long ago emptied of song,
Keep watch for resurrections.
Field wrens and meadowlarks
Gently flagellate the still air;

Their elegiac wings
Are voices whispering musical eulogies
Over green, seething fields.
A cast-iron pump,
Stranded like a nameless statue

In the middle of this vast countryside,
Waits patiently for a shape
To remember it to its task.
I grasp its pitted handle
To see how much it's forgotten.

The water its spout finally speaks
Is an oracle deeply drawn
From souls sleeping below my feet.
As their words splash my flesh,
I realize they're alive today,

Yet choose to withhold judgment
On those still too busy dying;
They thrive on silence in wet soil
Where their seeds, though planted
In a hundred different seasons,

Keep growing older each year
Without really growing at all.
My eyes gather in their names and dates
As part of the sweetest harvest
Ever taken from this land.

And as I stand out here alone,
Their blood circulating through my veins,
My heart renews acquaintanceships
Made in an ancient time
With tillers of the Tribe of Abraham.

The Drift of Things

> Ah, when to the heart of man
>   Was it ever less than a treason
> To go with the drift of things,
>   To yield with a grace to reason,
> And bow and accept the end
>   Of a love or a season?
>   "Reluctance" — Robert Frost

All along West Columbia Street
Ageless swaying patriarchs,
Like drawn slings flinging wingèd shot,
Release their weights to the breeze.

My wincing eyes can't quite accommodate
Such stinging ecstasy,
Or ears distinguish death's groan
From the singing of flown, transcendent things.

Instead, like a numb pallbearer
Stranded in this middle zone
Of brittle husks, shadows, stunted grass,
I bury the passing season without complaint.

Suddenly, a butterfly,
Clinging precipitously to a cider press
At the edge of its existence,
Beats its quivering wings

And, buffeted like a salmon leaping upstream,
Lifts amidst fluttering leaves.
Asserting independence of earth, soaring,
It indicts my senses for treason.

Redbuds

My excited eyes take me by the hand,
Lead me through a pure fuchsia net
Of redbuds yawning and stretching into bloom.
We awaken each other with our subtle touching

As I pass from one room to another
Within this open-air greenhouse.
Apple trees and dogwoods arouse me
To taste their lacy white fragrance; I linger,

Stop long enough to memorize their scent,
Then continue along the labyrinthian path
My eyes cut through winter's debris.

Everywhere in April's aquamarine sea,
Along whose lee shore I leisurely loaf,
Clipper ships, frigates, and whaling packets
Rolling in irons this early springtide

Begin lifting green sails up masts,
Prepare to raise anchor for summer oceans.
I wave to invisible crews, active as bees
Aboard the mind's fleet, and secretly contrive

A means of stowing away, securing release
From the land-locked harbor where my spirit
Has lain in dry dock too long.

But no escape outlines its design on my irises;
Yet, as I retreat from daydreams,
My feet going toward this new season,
I realize freedom requires little more

Than rediscovering life cycles
That connect us to each other, and each
To original Creation. Survival depends on eyes
Apprehending future and past in the universal Now;

They alone can sow seeds, plant the soul
In fertile earth, fuse bones with air:
Mine is the blood of the redbud tree.

Breaking Through

A Loirelike shimmer
Rims this Mississippi River valley
Through which my vehicle spins.
Never have such vibrant greens
Entranced my eyes to listen to prophecies
Spoken by sweet corn
Breaking virgin, furrowed hymens

Or coaxed me to envision fibrous stalks
Tightening like slender strings
Around skypegs fastened to a lyre
Whose cosmic vibrations
Connect me with all things
Procreated, germinating,
Or about to rise spontaneously.

Awakening from reverie, I realize
Just being here another season
Is the only natural magic
My winter-weary mind requires
For drawing back its ground cover
And finding itself in time,
Alive, in love with life, my heart its child!

The Flower Store

For Margaret, Harry F.,
and Mamo Hofmann

The thick, purple scent of hyacinth clusters
Saturates my nose and eyes
As though they were growing inside my head.
A wine-dark gloxinia,
Floating on the marble floor
Beside kalanchoes and potted mums,
Is a genuflecting nun in velvet robes
Attracting me to holiness by its silent repose.

In this land where unfragranced imitations —
Silk flowers and plastic plants,
Inanimate amidst the living —
Also wait to be given purpose
By creative hands,
I stand on the edge of inspiration,
Gazing through opaque drowsiness
Into mirrors multiplying visions of God.

Suddenly, I see myself blossoming,
Somewhere between Genesis and Eternity.

LOUIS DANIEL BRODSKY

Louis Daniel Brodsky was born in St. Louis, Missouri, in 1941, where he attended St. Louis Country Day School. After earning a B.A., Magna Cum Laude, at Yale University in 1963, he received an M.A. in English from Washington University in 1967 and an M.A. in Creative Writing from San Francisco State University in 1968.

Mr. Brodsky is the author of fourteen volumes of poetry. In addition, he has published nine scholarly books on Nobel laureate William Faulkner, including *William Faulkner, Life Glimpses*.

Listing his occupation as Poet, he is also an adjunct instructor at Mineral Area College in Flat River, Missouri, and Curator of the Brodsky Faulkner Collection at Southeast Missouri State University in Cape Girardeau, Missouri.

4249